# MIGRAINE DIET

# 40+ Stew, roast and casserole recipes for a healthy and balanced migraine diet

# TABLE OF CONTENTS

This document is geared towards providing exact and reliable information in regards to the topic and issue covered. The publication is sold with the idea that the publisher is not required to render accounting, officially permitted, or otherwise, qualified services. If advice is necessary, legal or professional, a practiced individual in the profession should be ordered.

- From a Declaration of Principles which was accepted and approved equally by a Committee of the American Bar Association and a Committee of Publishers and Associations.

Introduction

Migraine recipes for personal enjoyment but also for family enjoyment. You will love them for sure for how easy it is to prepare them.

## ROASTED SQUASH

Serves:      **3-4**

Prep Time:   **10**   Minutes

Cook Time:   **20**   Minutes

Total Time:  **30**   Minutes

### INGREDIENTS

- 2 delicata squashes
- 2 tablespoons olive oil
- 1 tsp curry powder
- 1 tsp salt

### DIRECTIONS

1. Preheat the oven to 400 F
2. Cut everything in half lengthwise
3. Toss everything with olive oil and place onto a prepared baking sheet
4. Roast for 18-20 minutes at 400 F or until golden brown
5. When ready remove from the oven and serve

# ROASTED CARROT

Serves: **3-4**

Prep Time: **10** Minutes

Cook Time: **20** Minutes

Total Time: **30** Minutes

## INGREDIENTS

- 1 lb. carrot
- 2 tablespoons olive oil
- 1 tsp curry powder
- 1 tsp salt

## DIRECTIONS

1. Preheat the oven to 400 F
2. Cut everything in half lengthwise
3. Toss everything with olive oil and place onto a prepared baking sheet
4. Roast for 18-20 minutes at 400 F or until golden brown
5. When ready remove from the oven and serve

## ZUCCHINI SOUP

Serves:        *4*

Prep Time:   *10*   Minutes

Cook Time:   *20*   Minutes

Total Time:   *30*   Minutes

### INGREDIENTS

- 1 tablespoon olive oil
- 1 lb. zucchini
- ¼ red onion
- ½ cup all-purpose flour
- ¼ tsp salt
- ¼ tsp pepper
- 1 can vegetable broth
- 1 cup heavy cream

### DIRECTIONS

1. In a saucepan heat olive oil and sauté zucchini until tender
2. Add remaining ingredients to the saucepan and bring to a boil
3. When all the vegetables are tender transfer to a blender and blend until smooth
4. Pour soup into bowls, garnish with parsley and serve

## CHICKEN NUGGETS

Serves:        **3**

Prep Time:   **10**   Minutes

Cook Time:  **25**   Minutes

Total Time:  **35**   Minutes

### INGREDIENTS

- 2 chicken breasts
- ¼ cup almond flour
- 1 tablespoon seasoning
- 1 tablespoon olive oil
- ½ tsp salt
- ¼ tsp pepper

### DIRECTIONS

1. Preheat the oven to 375 F
2. In a bowl add seasoning, salt, almond flour, pepper
3. Add pieces of chicken breast into your bowl and cover with flour
4. Transfer to your baking sheet
5. Bake 18-20 minutes, remove and serve

# BEEF FAJITAS

Serves:        **3**

Prep Time:   **10**   Minutes

Cook Time:   **20**   Minutes

Total Time:   **30**   Minutes

## INGREDIENTS

- 1 lb. beef stir-fry strips
- 1 red onion
- 1 red bell pepper
- ¼ tsp tsp cumin
- ¼ tsp chili powder
- salt
- pepper
- 1 avocado

## DIRECTIONS

1. In a skillet add strips and stir-fry, add salt, pepper and cook for 2-3 minute and set aside
2. Add onions, bell peppers, chili powder, cumin and fry for 2-3 minutes
3. Remove to a plate and serve with avocado

# SUMMER SALMON

Serves:        *4*

Prep Time:    *10*    Minutes

Cook Time:    *30*    Minutes

Total Time:   *40*    Minutes

## INGREDIENTS

- 3 salmon fillets
- 2 leeks
- 6 oz. asparagus spears
- 1 cup sugar snap peas
- 3 tablespoons white wine
- 1 cup vegetable broth
- 1 tablespoon chives
- salt

## DIRECTIONS

1. In a Dutch oven add salmon, asparagus, wine, peas, chicken bean and pepper
2. Bring to boil and simmer for 12-15 minutes
3. Sprinkle with chives and serve

# GRILLED SALMON

Serves:          **4**

Prep Time:    **10**   Minutes

Cook Time:   **20**   Minutes

Total Time:   **30**   Minutes

## INGREDIENTS

- Juice of 1 lime
- 2 tablespoons basil
- 3 salmon fillets
- 2 tablespoons salmon fillets
- 2 cup low-fat yogurt
- 1 tablespoon mayonnaise

   ½ tsp lime zest
- salt
- mixed salad leaves

## DIRECTIONS

1. In a bowl mix pepper, basil, lime juice, salt and pepper
2. Add salmon fillets and let it marinade for 20-30 minutes
3. In another bowl mix lime zest, basil, mayonnaise, yogurt and salt
4. Preheat the oven to 400 F and place the salmon fillets on a ridged grill pan

5. Brush the salmon with marinade and grill for 4-5 minutes per side

6. When ready remove and serve

# MONKFISH MUSSEL KEBABS

Serves:        **12**
Prep Time:     **10**  Minutes

Cook Time:     **20**  Minutes

Total Time:    **30**  Minutes

## INGREDIENTS

- 1 lemon
- juice 1 lime
- 1 tablespoon olive oil
- 1 tsp honey
- 1 garlic clove
- 1 tablespoon oregano
- 1 tablespoon parsley
- 6 oz. monkfish fillet
- 12 fresh mussels
- 1 yellow bell pepper
- 1 zucchini
- 12 cherry tomatoes
- salt

## DIRECTIONS

1. In a bowl add lime juice, honey, lemon zest, garlic, oregano and salt and mix well, marinade for 50-60 minutes
2. Prepare 10-12 wooden skewers and add on each one skewer 1 cube of monkfish, 1 piece of bell pepper, 1 zucchini, 1 mussel and a cherry tomato
3. Grill each kebab for 10-12 minutes or until done
4. When ready, remove and serve

# POTATO TORTILLA

Serves:        **6**

Prep Time:   **10**   Minutes

Cook Time:   **20**   Minutes

Total Time:  **30**   Minutes

## INGREDIENTS

- 1,5 lb. potatoes
- 1 tablespoon olive oil
- 1 red onion
- 1 zucchini
- 1 slice turkey bacon
- 5 eggs
- 1 tablespoon parsley
- pepper

## DIRECTIONS

1. In a saucepan add potato cubes, water and bring to a boil
2. In a skillet add potatoes, bacon, zucchini and cook until potatoes are tender
3. In a bowl beat the eggs, add water, pepper, parsley, pour the egg mixture over the vegetables and cook for 4-5 minutes
4. Slide the tortilla onto a plate, cool for 2-3 minutes and cut into wedges and serve

# ASIAN STIR-FRY

Serves:         **2**

Prep Time:   **10**   Minutes

Cook Time:  **10**   Minutes

Total Time:  **20**   Minutes

### INGREDIENTS

- ½ lb. dried noodles
- 1 lb. Asian stir-fry vegetables
- ½ cups hoisin sauce
- 1 tsp chili flakes

### DIRECTIONS

1. **In a frying pan add vegetables, water and stir-fry for 4-5 minutes**
2. **Add hoisin sauce, noodles, chili flakes and toss to coat, remove and serve**

# APRICOT CHICKEN PATTIES

Serves:          **4**

Prep Time:    **10**   Minutes

Cook Time:    **10**   Minutes

Total Time:    **20**   Minutes

## INGREDIENTS

- 1 lb. chicken mince
- 2 slices bread
- 3 oz. pistachio nuts
- 1/3 lb. dried apricots

## DIRECTIONS

1. In a bowl mix combine the mince, apricots, bread, pistachios and season with pepper
2. Roll into o4 patties and cook for 4-5 minutes per side
3. Remove and serve

# GREEN PESTO PASTA

Serves:        2
Prep Time:     5    Minutes

Cook Time:    15    Minutes

Total Time:   20    Minutes

## INGREDIENTS

- 4 oz. spaghetti
- 2 cups basil leaves
- 2 garlic cloves
- ¼ cup olive oil
- 2 tablespoons parmesan cheese
- ½ tsp black pepper

## DIRECTIONS

1. Bring water to a boil and add pasta
2. In a blend add parmesan cheese, basil leaves, garlic and blend
3. Add olive oil, pepper and blend again
4. Pour pesto onto pasta and serve when ready

# SALMON WITH ROSEMAY

Serves:      **2**

Prep Time:  **10**  Minutes

Cook Time:  **10**  Minutes

Total Time:  **20**  Minutes

## INGREDIENTS

- 3 Atlantic salmon fillets
- 2 tsp olive oil
- 1 clove garlic
- 1 tablespoon rosemary
- black pepper
- 1 tablespoon lemon juice
- 1 tablespoon white wine

## DIRECTIONS

1. In a frying pan sauté garlic, rosemary and pepper for 1-2 minutes
2. Add fish and cook for 1-2 minutes per side

# MUSHROOM BURGERS

Serves:          **2**

Prep Time:     **10**   Minutes

Cook Time:    **10**   Minutes

Total Time:    **20**   Minutes

## INGREDIENTS

- 2 tablespoons olive oil
- 1 lb. mushrooms
- 1 lb. beef mince
- 1 onion
- 1 tsp Worcestershire sauce
- 1 egg
- 4 hamburger buns
- 1 cup lettuce
- 4 slices tomatoes
- salt

## DIRECTIONS

1. In a frying pan add mushrooms and cook for 4-5 minutes, remove and set aside
2. In a bowl mix beef mince, salt, pepper, Worcestershire sauce, mushrooms, onion and mix well
3. Form into 2 patties, and refrigerate for 10-15 minutes

4. In a frying pan cook patty for 2-3 minutes per side and also grill hamburger buns

5. Top buns with lettuce, tomatoes and patties

6. Serve when ready

# BLACK BEANS BURGERS

Serves:        **4**

Prep Time:    **10**   Minutes

Cook Time:    **20**   Minutes

Total Time:   **30**   Minutes

## INGREDIENTS

- 1 lb. black beans
- 1 cup brown rice
- 1 onion
- 1 onion
- ¼ tsp tabasco sauce
- 1 egg
- ½ cup bread crumbs
- 5 tablespoons salsa
- 4 hamburger buns
- ½ cups yoghurt
- 4 leaves romaine lettuce
- 1 avocado

## DIRECTIONS

1. **Preheat the oven to 325 F**

2. In a bowl mix mashed beans, onions, tabasco sauce, rice, egg, breadcrumbs and mix well

3. Divide mixture into patties and bake for 12-15 minutes or until done

4. In another bowl mix yoghurt and salsa, serve with lettuce and avocado

# CABBAGE FRITATTA

Serves:        **2**

Prep Time:     **10**   Minutes

Cook Time:     **20**   Minutes

Total Time:    **30**   Minutes

## INGREDIENTS

- ½ lb. cabbage
- 1 tablespoon olive oil
- ½ red onion
- 2 eggs
- ¼ tsp salt
- 2 oz. cheddar cheese
- 1 garlic clove
- ¼ tsp dill

## DIRECTIONS

1. In a bowl whisk eggs with salt and cheese
2. In a frying pan heat olive oil and pour egg mixture
3. Add remaining ingredients and mix well
4. Serve when ready

# BRUSSEL SPROUTS FRITATTA

Serves:        **2**

Prep Time:   **10**  Minutes

Cook Time:  **20**  Minutes

Total Time:  **30**  Minutes

## INGREDIENTS

- ½ lb. Brussel sprouts
- 1 tablespoon olive oil
- ½ red onion
- ¼ tsp salt
- 2 eggs
- 2 oz. cheddar cheese
- 1 garlic clove
- ¼ tsp dill

## DIRECTIONS

1. In a skillet sauté Brussel sprouts until tender
2. In a bowl whisk eggs with salt and cheese
3. In a frying pan heat olive oil and pour egg mixture
4. Add remaining ingredients and mix well
5. Serve when ready

# CELERY FRITATTA

Serves:        **2**

Prep Time:   **10**   Minutes

Cook Time:  **20**   Minutes

Total Time:  **30**   Minutes

## INGREDIENTS

- 1 cup celery
- 1 tablespoon olive oil
- ½ red onion
- ¼ tsp salt
- 2 eggs
- 2 oz. cheddar cheese
- 1 garlic clove
- ¼ tsp dill

## DIRECTIONS

1. In a bowl whisk eggs with salt and cheese
2. In a frying pan heat olive oil and pour egg mixture
3. Add remaining ingredients and mix well
4. When ready serve with sautéed celery

# PROSCIUTTO FRITATTA

Serves:          **2**
Prep Time:   **10**   Minutes

Cook Time:   **20**   Minutes

Total Time:   **30**   Minutes

## INGREDIENTS

- 8-10 slices prosciutto
- 1 tsp rosemary
- 1 tablespoon olive oil
- ½ red onion
- ¼ tsp salt
- 2 eggs
- 2 oz. parmesan cheese
- 1 garlic clove
- ¼ tsp dill

## DIRECTIONS

1. In a bowl whisk eggs with salt and parmesan cheese
2. In a frying pan heat olive oil and pour egg mixture
3. Add remaining ingredients and mix well
4. When prosciutto and eggs are cooked remove from heat and serve

# OREGANO FRITATTA

Serves:        *2*

Prep Time:    *10*   Minutes

Cook Time:    *20*   Minutes

Total Time:   *30*   Minutes

## INGREDIENTS

- 1 tsp oregano
- 1 tablespoon olive oil
- ½ red onion
- ¼ tsp salt
- 2 eggs
- 2 oz. cheddar cheese
- 1 garlic clove
- ¼ tsp dill

## DIRECTIONS

1. In a bowl whisk eggs with salt and cheese
2. In a frying pan heat olive oil and pour egg mixture
3. Add remaining ingredients and mix well
4. Serve when ready

# HUMMUS WRAP

Serves:        **2**

Prep Time:     **5**    Minutes

Cook Time:     **5**    Minutes

Total Time:    **10**   Minutes

## INGREDIENTS

- 1 cup cooked brown rice
- 1 gluten-free tortilla
- 2-3 tablespoons hummus
- ¼ cup black beans
- ¼ cup tomatoes
- ¼ cup cucumber
- ¼ cup avocado
- ¼ cup romaine lettuce

## DIRECTIONS

1. Microwave the tortilla for 20-30 seconds
2. Spread hummus on tortilla
3. Add beans, tomatoes, cucumber, and remaining ingredients
4. Roll like a burrito and serve

# POTATO WEDGES

Serves: **4-6**

Prep Time: **10** Minutes

Cook Time: **30** Minutes

Total Time: **40** Minutes

## INGREDIENTS

- 2 white potatoes
- 1 tsp olive oil
- 1 tsp garlic powder
- 1 tsp onion powder
- salt
- 1 cup avocado dip

## DIRECTIONS

1. Slice potatoes into thick slices
2. In a bowl combine garlic powder, onion powder, salt, olive oil and mix well
3. Place the potatoes into the mixture and stir to coat
4. Bake the potatoes at 425 F for 25-30 minutes
5. When ready remove from the oven and serve with avocado dip

# KALE CHIPS

Serves:        **4**

Prep Time:   **10**   Minutes

Cook Time:   **15**   Minutes

Total Time:   **25**   Minutes

## INGREDIENTS

- 2 cups kale
- 1 tablespoon avocado oil
- 1 tsp salt
- 1 tsp turmeric
- 1 tsp chili powder
- 1 tsp curry powder

## DIRECTIONS

1. In a bowl combine all ingredients except kale
2. Mix well and add kale to the seasoning mixture
3. Toss to coat and then place the kale in a baking dish
4. Bake at 250 F for 12-15 minutes
5. When ready remove from the oven and serve

# EGG ROLL BOWL

Serves:         *2*
Prep Time:   *10*   Minutes

Cook Time:   *20*   Minutes

Total Time:   *30*   Minutes

## INGREDIENTS

- 1 tablespoon olive oil
- 1 clove garlic
- 1 lb. pork
- ½ red onion
- 1 cup carrot
- 1 cabbage
- ½ cup soy sauce
- ¼ tsp black pepper

## DIRECTIONS

1. In a skillet sauté garlic and onion until soft
2. Add pork, cabbage and cook for another 6-7 minutes
3. Add soy sauce, carrot and cook until vegetables are tender
4. When ready transfer mixture to a bowl, add pepper and serve

# GREEK BOWL

Serves: **1**

Prep Time: **10** Minutes

Cook Time: **20** Minutes

Total Time: **30** Minutes

## INGREDIENTS

- 1 tablespoon olive oil
- 1 chicken breast
- 1 tsp oregano
- 1 tsp black pepper
- 1 cup tomatoes
- ¼ cucumber
- ¼ cup red onion
- ¼ cup black olives
- 1/4 cup feta cheese
- 1 cup dressing

## DIRECTIONS

1. In a skillet add chicken and cook until golden
2. Add seasoning and onion
3. When ready place all ingredients in a bowl
4. Drizzle dressing on top, mix well and serve

# CRANBERRY SALAD

Serves:         2
Prep Time:    5    Minutes

Cook Time:   15   Minutes

Total Time:   20   Minutes

## INGREDIENTS

- ½ cup celery
- 1 packet Knox Gelatin
- 1 cup cranberry juice
- 1 can berry cranberry sauce
- 1 cup sour cream

## DIRECTIONS

1. In a pan add juice, gelatin, cranberry sauce and cook on low heat
2. Add sour cream, celery and continue to cook
3. Pour mixture into a pan
4. Serve when ready

# GAZPACHO SALAD

Serves:        **4**
Prep Time:    **10**   Minutes

Cook Time:    **30**   Minutes

Total Time:   **40**   Minutes

## INGREDIENTS

- ½ lb. cherry tomatoes
- ½ cucumber
- 3 oz. cooked quinoa
- 1 tsp bouillon powder
- 2 spring onions
- 1 red pepper
- ½ avocado
- 1 pack Japanese tofu

## DIRECTIONS

1. In a bowl combine all ingredients together
2. Add salad dressing, toss well and serve

Serves:        **4**
Prep Time:    **10**   Minutes

Cook Time:    **30**   Minutes

Total Time:    **40**   Minutes

## INGREDIENTS

- 1 tsp olive oil
- ¼ lb. tomatoes
- 2 oz. radish
- 1 oz. parsley
- 1 tablespoon coriander
- salt

## DIRECTIONS

1. In a bowl combine all ingredients together and mix well
2. Add salad dressing, toss well and serve

# ZUCCHINI & BELL PEPPER SALAD

Serves:       *1*
Prep Time:    *5*    Minutes

Cook Time:    *5*    Minutes

Total Time:   *10*   Minutes

## INGREDIENTS

- ¼ cup zucchini
- ¼ cup red capsicum
- ½ cup yellow capsicum
- 1 cup sprouted moong
- ¼ cup apple
- 1 tablespoon olive oil
- 1 tsp lemon juice

## DIRECTIONS

1. In a bowl combine all ingredients together and mix well
2. Add olive oil, toss well and serve

# QUINOA & AVOCADO SALAD

Serves:         *1*

Prep Time:    *5*    Minutes

Cook Time:   *5*    Minutes

Total Time:   *10*    Minutes

## INGREDIENTS

- ¼ cooked quinoa
- ¼ cup avocado
- ¼ cup zucchini
- ¼ cup capsicum cubes
- ¼ cup mushroom
- ½ cup cherry tomatoes
- 1 cup lettuce
- 1 tablespoon sprouts
- 1 tsp olive oil
- Salad dressing

## DIRECTIONS

1. In a bowl combine all ingredients together and mix well
2. Add salad dressing, toss well and serve

# TOFU SALAD

Serves: **1**

Prep Time: **5** Minutes

Cook Time: **5** Minutes

Total Time: **10** Minutes

## INGREDIENTS

- 1 pack tofu
- 1 cup chopped vegetables (carrots, cucumber)

## DRESSING

- 1 tablespoon sesame oil
- 1 tablespoon mustard
  1 tablespoon brown rice vinegar
- 1 tablespoon soya sauce

## DIRECTIONS

1. In a bowl combine all ingredients together and mix well
2. Add salad dressing, toss well and serve

# PAD THAI SALAD

Serves: **1**

Prep Time: **5** Minutes

Cook Time: **5** Minutes

Total Time: **10** Minutes

## INGREDIENTS

- ¼ lb. rice noodles
- 1 red pepper
- 1 onion
- 4 stalks coriander
- ¼ package silken tofu
- 1 oz. roasted peanuts
- Salad dressing

## DIRECTIONS

1. In a bowl combine all ingredients together and mix well
2. Add salad dressing, toss well and serve

# AVOCADO SALAD

Serves: **1**

Prep Time: **5** Minutes

Cook Time: **5** Minutes

Total Time: **10** Minutes

## INGREDIENTS

- 2 avocados
- ¼ lb. snap peas
- 1 tablespoon sesame seeds

## SALAD DRESSING

- 1 tablespoon soya sauce
- 1 tablespoon umeboshi puree
- 2 tablespoons mikawa mirin

## DIRECTIONS

1. In a bowl combine all ingredients together and mix well
2. Add salad dressing, toss well and serve

# MUSHROOM SALAD

Serves:        *1*
Prep Time:    5   Minutes

Cook Time:    5   Minutes

Total Time:   *10*   Minutes

### INGREDIENTS

- ½ lb. mushrooms
- 1 clove garlic
- ½ lb. salad leaves
- ¼ lb. tofu
- 1 oz. walnuts
- salad dressing

### DIRECTIONS

1. In a bowl combine all ingredients together and mix well
2. Add salad dressing, toss well and serve

# MIXED GREENS SALAD

Serves:         **1**
Prep Time:      **5**    Minutes

Cook Time:      **5**    Minutes

Total Time:     **10**   Minutes

## INGREDIENTS

- 2 cucumbers
- 3 radishes
- ¼ red bell pepper
- 2 spring onions
- 1 tablespoon red wine vinegar
- 1 tablespoon rice vinegar
- 1 tablespoon soya sauce
- 1 tablespoon clearspring mirin
- 2 cups mixed salad greens

## DIRECTIONS

1. In a bowl combine all ingredients together and mix well
2. Add salad dressing, toss well and serve

# QUINOA SALAD

Serves:        **1**

Prep Time:     **5**    Minutes

Cook Time:     **5**    Minutes

Total Time:    **10**   Minutes

## INGREDIENTS

- 1 cup cooked quinoa
- ¼ cup clearspring hijiki
- ¼ red bell pepper
- 1 bun watercress
- 2 radishes
- 2 tablespoons goji berries

## DIRECTIONS

1. In a bowl combine all ingredients together and mix well
2. Add salad dressing, toss well and serve

## FISH STEW

Serves:         **4**

Prep Time:   **15**   Minutes

Cook Time:   **45**   Minutes

Total Time:   **60**   Minutes

### INGREDIENTS

- 1 fennel bulb
- 1 red onion
- 2 garlic cloves
- 2 tablespoons olive oil
- 1 cup white wine
- 1 tablespoon fennel seeds
- 4 bay leaves
- 2 cups chicken stock
- 8 oz. halibut
- 12 oz. haddock

### DIRECTIONS

1. Chop all ingredients in big chunks
2. In a large pot heat olive oil and add ingredients one by one

3. Cook for 5-6 or until slightly brown
4. Add remaining ingredients and cook until tender, 35-45 minutes
5. Season while stirring on low heat
6. When ready remove from heat and serve

# BUTTERNUT SQUASH STEW

Serves:          **4**

Prep Time:     **15**   Minutes

Cook Time:    **45**   Minutes

Total Time:   **60**   Minutes

## INGREDIENTS

- 2 tablespoons olive oil
- 2 red onions
- 2 cloves garlic
- 1. Tablespoon rosemary
- 1 tablespoon thyme
- 2 lb. beef
- 1 cup white wine
- 1 cup butternut squash
- 2 cups beef broth
- ½ cup tomatoes
-

## DIRECTIONS

1. Chop all ingredients in big chunks
2. In a large pot heat olive oil and add ingredients one by one
3. Cook for 5-6 or until slightly brown
4. Add remaining ingredients and cook until tender, 35-45 minutes

5. Season while stirring on low heat

6. When ready remove from heat and serve

## BACON CASSEROLE

Serves:        **4**

Prep Time:    **10**   Minutes

Cook Time:    **15**   Minutes

Total Time:   **25**   Minutes

### INGREDIENTS

- 4-5 slices bacon
- 3-4 tablespoons butter
- 5-6 tablespoons flour
- 2 cups milk
- 3 cups cheddar cheese
- 2 cups chicken breast
- 1 tsp seasoning mix

### DIRECTIONS

1. Sauté the veggies and set aside
2. Preheat the oven to 425 F
3. Transfer the sautéed veggies to a baking dish, add remaining ingredients to the baking dish
4. Mix well, add seasoning and place the dish in the oven
5. Bake for 12-15 minutes or until slightly brown

6. When ready remove from the oven and serve

# ENCHILADA CASSEROLE

Serves:         **4**

Prep Time:    **10**   Minutes

Cook Time:   **25**   Minutes

Total Time:   **35**   Minutes

## INGREDIENTS

- 1 tablespoon olive oil
- 1 red onion
- 1 bell pepper
- 2 cloves garlic
- 1 can black beans
- 1 cup chicken
- 1 can green chilis
- 1 can enchilada sauce
- 1 cup cheddar cheese
- 1 cup sour cream

## DIRECTIONS

1. Sauté the veggies and set aside
2. Preheat the oven to 425 F
3. Transfer the sautéed veggies to a baking dish, add remaining ingredients to the baking dish

4. Mix well, add seasoning and place the dish in the oven
5. Bake for 15-25 minutes or until slightly brown
6. When ready remove from the oven and serve

## CASSEROLE PIZZA

Serves:         **6-8**

Prep Time:   **10**   Minutes

Cook Time:   **15**   Minutes

Total Time:   **25**   Minutes

### INGREDIENTS

- 1 pizza crust
- ½ cup tomato sauce
- ¼ black pepper
- 1 cup zucchini slices
- 1 cup mozzarella cheese
- 1 cup olives

### DIRECTIONS

1. Spread tomato sauce on the pizza crust
2. Place all the toppings on the pizza crust
3. Bake the pizza at 425 F for 12-15 minutes
4. When ready remove pizza from the oven and serve

*THANK YOU FOR READING THIS BOOK!*

CPSIA information can be obtained
at www.ICGtesting.com
Printed in the USA
BVHW040821111120
592842BV00031B/575